PROJECT FAILURES ARE KILLING US!

PRIORITIES FOR REMOVING THE RISK FROM PROJECT MANAGEMENT!

ROBERT L. NITSCHKE

MAPCATA Publishing
23121 102nd Pl. W
Edmonds, WA 98020
Ph 425-478-1911

10 9 8 7 6 5 4 3 2 1

Printed in the United States of America

ISBN-10 1482007770

ISBN-13 978-1482007770

Cover designer: WebDesignsGURU
Typographer: Stephanie Martindale
Editing/Mentor: Carl Levi, PowerProof LLC

Puzzle © Missjelena | Dreamstime.com

This book is dedicated to my very understanding and supportive wife Barb who is not only my life supporter but my very important business partner; to my children and grandchildren who are a joy to be with; to my business colleagues and clients who have been so supportive and receptive to my words; and to those leaders that continue to receive the disturbing news time after time that their projects are not performing to plan.

CONTENTS

PREFACE

As I sit in the air-cushioned executive chair around the board-room-style table that is surrounded by 11 companion look-alike chairs, I am anxious about what the project team members filing into the room are about to tell me.

They are not looking at me; which is never a good sign. It feels just like last week's meeting at this same time. I am preparing myself for the worst as I set my feet under the table, open my project task list and raise my eyes to see who is brave enough to acknowledge that I am sitting here at the end of the table.

Who will voluntarily deliver the news first? As I look at each of them, I can tell that no one wants to speak! Again, not a good sign.

Two and half hours of listening to excuses for who did not do what, when, or where—but not WHY, another project review meeting comes to a close. Once again, it ends with an ever-growing list of not-started-yet, incompletes, not enough resources, and lots of I-don't-knows.

I walk away with only one notion in my head; "Another failure. Only this time, I am not going to let this trend continue; it is time to turn these project failures into successes. A change must be made, and it must be made NOW!

This book is based on 30 years of experience and an untold number of project review meeting setbacks. The content of this book—if applied to any project management situation—is GUARANTEED to reduce risk and create significant SUCCESS!

INTRODUCTION

The specialty of Project Management (PM) has evolved over the past two decades into an interdisciplinary activity that is increasingly gaining recognition as a critical success factor for any enterprise, whether for profit or non-profit. Hundreds of books, articles, seminars, and associations have been developed based on the Project Management discipline. The best known of these associations is the Project Management Institute (PMI), which has created an internationally recognized organization focusing on the teaching and certification of Project Management, with recent expansions to include Program Management, Risk Management, Scheduling, and Associate certifications for each of these major areas of study. Project Management Institute has developed a strong Project Management Book of Knowledge (PMBOK), which includes the techniques upon which its Project Management Certification process is based. With the recognition and formalization of the Project Management discipline within numerous enterprises, Project Management is developing into a career path for individuals wishing to extend specific expertise to satisfy the demands of the individual enterprise.

Business effectiveness is the stimulus for the increased awareness of the value that *successful* project management brings to the organization's bottom line. It is also the corporation that dictates the direction of Project Management as a discipline within the organization, either positively or not. The corporation establishes the formality and level of evolution of Project Management within the organization, and it must recognize that Project Management disciplines are needed in *every* aspect of its operation.

The term *Project Management* is most often associated with software development projects, and it is often incorrectly used interchangeably with *product* development projects. Let's try to clarify this confusion:

- **Product Development** can be defined as those activities required for developing a product or service, including requirements, design, construction, testing, and operating.

- **Project Management** is the *discipline used* during the product development project, including project definition (sponsorship, purpose, goals, controls), project planning (goals, strategies, tactics), and project control (measurement, risk management, change control, communication/reporting).

Project Management is the *means to an end*: the product or service.

Once the product is tested and operating (or ready for market), the project is complete if it has been properly closed out with the project team and stakeholders.

The Project Management discipline is pertinent in any project situation, including business processes, rules, software development, manufacturing products/processes, service products/processes, and organizational development/human resource process, just to name a few. Project Management methods or techniques should be applied at all levels of the organization, no matter how insignificant or unsophisticated the project or activity may seem. Project Management is a flexible discipline and should be tailored to the organization and/or the project needs. After all, the objective of Project Management is to complete a project successfully.

Just what constitutes a successful project? It can be defined as an activity that has a beginning and an end that meet the sponsor's expectation by delivering the desired results within an acceptable budget and time objective.

Why do organizations struggle with a *less than effective* Project Management discipline within their organizations? The simple answer is that at most corporate Project Management disciplines have evolved over time and have not actually been planned. The enterprise culture has a significant impact on how the organization operates, and that includes how effectively the company conducts its Project Management process. If an organization recognizes that it is time to re-evaluate its Project Management discipline and move forward to make it more effective, then they should consider a new perspective. *Knowing the priorities needed for effective Project Management may make the difference between more-of-the-same and a real, tangible change.*

PRIORITIES -
A NEW PERSPECTIVE

The corporate leadership (Chief Executive Officer, President, Chief Financial Officer, and Chief Operating Officer) has a fiduciary responsibility to ensure that the organization is operating in the most effective manner to generate the best possible long-term returns to its owners (shareholders/investors). Having the strong support of the executive-level management team involved in evaluating the organization's commitments – and steering the move toward a more effective Project Management discipline within the enterprise are critical.

Most small to medium size enterprises (20-500 employees) continue to conduct Project Management as they have from the beginning of time. The Project Management discipline has evolved based on the people that have been involved in projects, and their methods were based on their background, experience, and expertise. Some organizations have done a very good job of training, planning, and moving the Project Management discipline forward, but they are in a minority. Since several surveys have reflected a 60%-70% failure rate for projects costing billions of dollars in real or opportunity costs and lost revenues, it is easy to see why a business's Project Management discipline effectiveness level should be reviewed.

Those organizations whose approaches to increasing Project Management effectiveness consist of requiring all Project Managers to become Certified Project Managers will be extremely disappointed. Upgrading the knowledge of Project Managers is an advisable investment, but that change alone will not necessarily make the corporate Project Management discipline more effective nor will it ensure any greater success of their projects.

In recent years, some organizations have considered that the best way to achieve the goal of a more effective Project Management process would be to hire a consulting organization to implement a Project Management process and train their staff. This action in and of itself is not a poor strategy, but such decisions should be made within the context of a total plan that has been thoroughly thought through regarding the return on investment (ROI) to the company. Otherwise, the results are likely to be equally disappointing.

How should an enterprise review their Project Management discipline and begin to make changes leading to greater effectiveness? A new perspective on how to revamp the Project Management discipline within the organization is: Start with a review of the *priorities* to be focused on for a more effective Project Management discipline. Most enterprise managers would say that the *process or methodology* is the most important factor, but I disagree. My view of the correct order of priorities for evaluating and implementing an enterprise's Project Management discipline is as follows: *Leadership, Resources, Communications, Accountability,* and finally, *Process.*

PRIORITY ONE - LEADERSHIP

*L**eadership* is the most critical priority for an effective enter-prise's Project Management discipline. *Leadership* must be present at all levels of the organization and this priority extends to executive management, project sponsors, program managers, project managers, operating management, project team members, and even the customer. If there is a weakness in leadership at any of these levels of a project, there is an increased risk for project delays, cost over-runs, deliverable shortfalls, or a complete project failure – causing a project to be canceled. Most of the publications available on the subject of Project Management to date seem to be focused on process or methodology. I will address the subject of *process* later in this book under Priority Five; however, while I feel that process or methodology is very important to the Project Management discipline, I feel it is just *less* important than the other priorities covered in this book.

Effective leaders have an inherent ability to produce desired results in a very effective manner, no matter which position in the enterprise they hold. These leaders know how to identify weakness, how to take action, and how to follow up continually on the action they've taken to ensure that they achieve the desired results. They are both strategists and facilitators, and they know the difference between the two.

Let's make a somewhat challenging assumption that the corporate executives and operating management are leaders and that they are truly committed to the revamping of the Project Management discipline within their company. Let's focus on the leadership traits needed for the program and project managers and our project team members to be more effective in their responsibilities. You will see that there is an overlap in these traits with the other priorities explained later; the difference is that effective leaders know that these other priorities are their responsibility in order to achieve the desired objective or result. Successful leaders know that if they cannot get someone else to do what is needed, then *they* must do it themselves. The following useful leadership traits were compiled by the Santa Clara University and the Tom Peters Group:

- **Honest -** Display sincerity, integrity, and candor in all your actions. Deceptive behavior will not inspire trust.

- **Competent -** Base your actions on reason and moral principles. Do not make decisions based on childlike, emotional desires or feelings.

- **Forward-looking -** Set goals and have a vision of the future. This vision must be owned throughout the organization. Effective leaders envision what they want and how to get it. They habitually pick priorities stemming from their basic values.

- **Inspiring -** Display confidence in all that you do. By showing endurance in mental, physical, and spiritual stamina, you will inspire others to reach for new heights. Take charge when necessary.

- **Intelligent** - Read, study, and seek challenging assignments.

- **Fair-minded** - Show fair treatment to all people. Prejudice is the enemy of justice. Display empathy by being sensitive to the feelings, values, interests, and well-being of others.

- **Broad-minded** - Seek out diversity of staff and thought.

- **Courageous** - Have the perseverance to accomplish a goal, regardless of the seemingly insurmountable obstacles. Display a confident calmness when under stress.

- **Straightforward** - Use sound judgment to make good decisions at the right time.

- **Imaginative** - Make timely and appropriate changes in your thinking, plans, and methods. Show creativity by thinking of new and better goals, ideas, and solutions to problems. Be innovative!

Project Management participants – program managers, project managers, team members, and operations management – all focused on the project at hand – should possess as many of these traits as possible to increase the probability of completing the project successfully. No one is perfect, and to say that you can staff a project with everyone's possessing such leadership traits is not realistic. However, the lack of such traits should not prevent making *leadership* a priority.

Effective leaders will compensate for the absence of other skills and shortcomings of project team members; weakness in the leadership positions will only compound a project's issues and lead to frustration, missed milestones, and cost over-runs.

Several surveys that I have seen discussing project failures (cancellations, cost over-runs, missed deadlines, or other poor results) list as the causes of those failures poor communication, lack of attention to human or organizational aspects, poor project management, poor articulation of user requirements, inadequate attention to business needs and goals, and failure to involve users appropriately. These are all symptoms of the real problem: a failure of *Leadership*. Let's look at some Project Management disciplined leadership examples. This list is not intended to be all-inclusive but to provide some examples:

- *Program* and *Project* Management leaders must:

   - Accept responsibility for the *entire* portfolio of projects or specific project.

   - Develop relationships (not just communicate) with everyone on the project, including the sponsor, the team, the operations management and the customer.

   - Know that interpersonal skills are required to get the best from everyone on the project.

   - Develop a clear and detailed description of the project(s) to which everyone agrees.

   - Communicate in person and in writing (meetings, email, reports, etc.) with all levels of the project(s).

   - Hold everyone (including yourself) accountable for each one's performance on the project.

   - Anticipate problems or issues and work with the project team to determine resolutions.

   - Prevent scope creep –unrestrained changes or endless growth in a project's scope – and short cutting, unless the risks have been analyzed and agreed to by the team.

   - Follow the project plan that the team approved.

- Provide a positive environment in which the team will work. Be a good listener.

- Take the responsibility to resolve any and all conflicts.

- *Project* team member leaders must:

  - Know they are part of a team, not acting as individuals.

  - Recognize that their activities are critical to the success of the project and take them seriously.

  - Be willing to help other team members with their issues to move the project forward.

  - Communicate with project management and colleagues at all times.

  - Maintain "can-do" attitudes.

  - Stay focused on the project plan approved by the team.

  - Provide feedback on activities taken or to be taken.

  - Meet all milestones and provide all required status reporting on time.

  - Ask for help if needed – do not hesitate.

  - Don't take shortcuts or change the plan without Project Management approval.

  - Anticipate problems or issues in their work and address them with the team proactively.

  - Develop relationships with all members of their team(s).

      □   Take pride in their work and in helping others within the team.

Make sure that your project leadership positions are occupied by leaders. If you do not have any leaders, then hire them (permanent or using consulting resources). Look at the cost and the return on investment (ROI) you are targeting for the project. How much will leadership cost versus the potential loss for a failed or inadequate project result? Start training your prospective leaders and leverage your existing leadership by establishing a mentoring program. Finding project leaders is a difficult process, but those enterprises that have committed to a Project Management discipline *should* know that they have to be committed to hiring and developing program and project managers who are now or potentially strong leaders. That commitment should extend to project analysts, administrators, and as many of the personnel involved in projects as possible. In my opinion, *Leadership* is the number One Priority in the quest for an effective Project Management discipline.

PRIORITY TWO -
RESOURCES

Projects of any type and size have several things in common, and one of them is that they need *resources* to be completed. *Resources* include, for example, labor, plant and equipment, office supplies, raw materials, manufacturing components, design services, research and development, consulting, software applications and information technology hardware, external support services, and legal assistance . Once you have the leadership for a project, it must then be staffed and resourced in order to move forward.

However, if there are no resources, the project does not have much of a chance for success, does it? It is up to the leadership to formulate the project plan, which should outline the objective, define the deliverables and the duration, estimate the cost, identify the activities to be accomplished, categorize the resources needed, and estimate the ROI of the project. This information is used by executive management for project evaluation and approval or disapproval.

The type of project will determine the levels and kinds of resources needed in support of the project. An Enterprise Resource Planning (ERP) application implementation, or upgrade project, has different resource requirements than a proprietary software-development project, which is different from a manufacturing-process improvement project, which is different from a manufactured-product development project. Nevertheless, all projects do have one resource requirement in common, and that is labor. They all require people to support the project: the project team, operations personnel, vendors or suppliers, consultants, lobbyists, and customers. Other resources required will depend on the nature of the project.

Important factors to keep in mind when resourcing a project with labor, Information Technology hardware, software or applications, supplies, plant and equipment, etc., is that *quantity* and *quality* are equally important in arriving at an accurate estimate and a successful project overall. *Quantity* is relatively self-explanatory: having the right amount of resources in order to complete the project as planned. *Quality* is not as obvious to many project managers when resourcing a project. The old saying is true here: "You get what you pay for." There is a balance between cost and quality, and I always call this a *ROI balance*.

Dividing the quality benefit by the cost will give you a quality ROI measurement. If we are in need of a new piece of equipment for the project, the quality criteria should be: lead time, useable life, features, ease of use, maintenance periods, size, weight, power requirement, parts availability, etc. If we are resourcing labor, then the quality criteria are more personal than in the case when considering a piece of equipment or a software application, and they would include such criteria as: leadership, subject knowledge, technical skill, work ethic, team player, good communicator (verbal and written), interpersonal skills, relative experience, loyalty, and availability.

When staffing a Project Manager position, a typical mistake made by a hiring manager, is in not understanding or taking the time to consider quality. When staffing a project with either internal or external personnel, or especially when they are looking to outsource the Project Manager position, the company will often look for a Subject Matter Expert to fill the Project Manager position. Every project needs subject matter experts, and they usually come from the operating organizations within the enterprise or from outsourced consulting organizations specializing in the required knowledge base.

Subject matter experts are important to the team, but they are not as important to the Project Manager position. For example, if a corporation is implementing an Enterprise Resource Planning system, they need a Project Manager who understands the overall architecture of what is involved with Enterprise Resource Planning systems, as well as the impacts on the operating functions that contribute to the Enterprise Resource Planning systems functionality once implemented.

The Project Manager needs to know, within the requirements, how the enterprise's business rules are configured and processed, as well as the overall data-management requirements, but he or she does not need to know the inter-workings of the application software. In this example, the company should have operating staff that have been trained on the details of inter-workings of the application, and there should be vendor subject matter expert support from the application-development firm that sold the application to the enterprise.

Determining the level of resources needed in order to forecast the project cost (budget) and duration (time) requires some estimating –capability, which is a combination of art and science – and the method of estimation will depend on the project type and the business's current practice(s). The size and complexity of the project will have a bearing on the selection of the most appropriate estimating technique from among the several that are available.

Furthermore, a key factor for determining a *good* estimate is to know as much as possible about the project. A large enterprise will often estimate and fund a planning phase of a large and complex project. This is a sub-project that is intended to develop a detailed plan for the main project by determining the requirements, resources and estimated cost, and duration of the primary project. On the other hand, a small, less complicated project may be defined on an *ad hoc* (taking into account only the case at hand and no wider applications) basis for estimating purposes. .

Estimating techniques take many different forms, depending on the enterprise's culture and the project type. A few examples of estimating techniques are: Top-Down, Bottom-Up, Parametric, and Phase or Stages. A brief discussion of these techniques follows:

- **Top-Down** - A project has been given a total cost and/ or duration metric (months, days, hours) and then it is broken down to its lowest level of activities, where resources are required. The next step is to work out what percentage each activity represents in relationship to the total. This approach is also called *proportioning*. If the total project is $100,000 and an activity is thought to be 2% of the total cost, then that activity would be estimated at $2,000. The same principle applies when calculating a labor metric. If the total project is fore-casted to require 100 hours of programming time and an activity is estimated to take 10% of the total, then that activity is estimated to be 10 hours.

- **Bottom-Up** - This technique is the inverse of the Top-Down approach. It starts with the same detailed plan, reflecting the activities where resources are required; each activity is then estimated (cost, duration). At the end of the process, all activities are added to reach a total for the project. This process is the most complex and time consuming; however, it provides for the greatest level of accuracy.

- **Parametric** - A common unit of measure (cost, time period, etc.) is determined for the project. As with other methods, a detailed list of project activities that must be resourced is compiled, and this is followed by an estimation process utilizing a multiple of the common unit of measure for each activity. If a common unit of labor is eight hours, then an activity may be estimated to be five times eight (common unit) or 40 hours.

- **Phase or Stage** - A project is divided into phases or stages, and each phase is estimated using any of the earlier techniques. Each phase is evaluated as to whether or not to continue with the project – based on the performance of the past phase and the forecast for the next phase. This approach is usually used for very large projects with very long duration periods; because in such a case, the overall project becomes more manageable if it is divided into phases or stages.

Resources are the fuels that make the project engine run under the leadership of the Project Manager. Projects that fail due to poor resourcing are those that end up significantly over budget or extremely late. Very few projects end up exactly on budget and on time, but successful projects are completed within an acceptable margin (acceptable variance from plan) of success, as established by executive management and sponsors. For an effective Project Management discipline, *Resourcing* is our Priority number Two.

PRIORITY THREE -
COMMUNICATION

Most publications written about the Project Management discipline list communications as a very critical factor in the success of a project, and I agree. Some surveys show that poor project *communication* accounts for approximately 50%-60% of project failures. Proper *communication* takes time, discipline, and the establishment of rules and standards for the project team, including the sponsors and customers. *Communication* comes in two flavors, *formal* and *informal*.

- **Formal communication** relates to the distribution of written (paper, electronic) plans, minutes and notes, agendas, and status and variance reporting. Formal communication is important to projects to ensure that appropriate individuals are aware of an issue or status, and that there is a record of such issue/status and any actions taken.

- **Informal communication** relates to verbal, telephone, or electronic (e.g email, instant messaging, texting) discussions in a small group or one-on-one sidebar situations. Informal communications are used for clarification and gathering additional information that is for the benefit of a single individual or a very small group of team members. There is no need for a record of these conversations and there is little benefit to others that can be derived from distributing the information to the entire project team. Valuable information may come from an informal communication event that would be elevated to a formal event if it is found to be beneficial to those team members and stakeholders not present.

Valuable communication must be *timely, accurate,* and *relevant.*

Timely communications are received while the information is still useable to the recipient. It is frustrating to receive a notice of a meeting that is scheduled for the day you receive the invitation – or worst yet, the day after the meeting was held. The lead time for receipt of such information should be determined by what action must be taken on the information by the recipient. Knowing the recipients and their relationship to the information is the responsibility of the originator of the communication.

If the communication is informational only and does not require action, then recipients should be provided with at least two to three days lead time to review and further dispatch the communication appropriately. After all, they may want to initiate a reply. Sadly, if the topic is old news by the time their reply would arrive, the responder may feel the originator sent the communication to them as an after-thought.

Often, there is the need for a last minute communication to discuss an issue or activity that was unanticipated. When this happens, then the originator should reach out to each recipient directly to set up a meeting or to communicate the information in the timeliest manner.

Accurate communications mean that the information being communicated is factual and readable (good grammar, spelling, and formatting). The only way to ensure that the news you are going to include in a communication is factual is to research the sources of the information and then determine how to best present the material to others.

If you are the original source of the information, then the process is extremely simple – if you are truthful and complete. In the *old days*, it was thought that if something was in print, it was accurate and factual. That belief is far from the truth; and with the integration of the Internet into our daily lives, information should be more suspect than ever. *Project Manager's should always validate and verify the information they receive from members of their team before distribution in any form to any recipient.* Accuracy in the Project Management discipline is critical and must be protected at all levels.

Relevance of information communicated throughout the Project Management discipline is a matter of providing the proper information at the right time. Communicating information that is not relevant to the topic at hand or to the wrong recipient causes confusion and wastes time. Unfortunately, confusing communications may sidetrack a portion of the project if the recipient believes there is a change in direction or perhaps a difference of opinion regarding the resolution of an issue or an approach for completing project activities. Originators should review their communication from the recipients' perspectives. Do they have a need to know? How are they going to view what I say? Am I clear in what I am trying to convey? Have I clearly identified the reason for the communication? Have I made myself available to those who need clarifications? Don't communicate unless you have a reason to do so.

Meetings are generally the most widely used and often overused form of communication within the Project Management discipline. The primary reason for choosing to call a meeting is that the issues involved require two-way communication. Where feedback or input is needed, then having as many of the team members as possible, who are impacted by the issue, in a room together – in order to solicit their feedback – is beneficial.

Meetings can also be the largest time waster within the Project Management discipline. If you are looking to inform team members or other stakeholders on a one-way basis, then the use of a one-way distribution method for the information is more effective (written report, broadcast fax, email, website). The method and frequency of distributing information for each stakeholder group should be established in the planning stage of the project in the Communication Plan. If the communication is a collaboration of input or feedback from team members or stakeholders, then a meeting is a good forum to collect, validate, and verify the information to be disseminated later. The following points are a few simple guidelines for conducting effective meetings:

- Send an invitation and agenda to each person you want to attend the meeting. The agenda should include topics, responsible person, and an allotted amount of time for each issue. Give invitees at least a week's notice to reduce the potential for schedule conflicts. The larger the meeting, the longer lead time, as there is a greater chance for unresolvable schedule conflicts that may impact your meeting attendees.

- Meetings should always start and end on time.

- Review the agenda at the beginning of the meeting and appoint a gatekeeper from the attendees to enforce the agenda, while remaining somewhat flexible.

- Appoint a secretary of the meeting. This is someone who takes minutes or notes as to the decisions made or significant points covered that are important to the project and to the team members and stakeholders.

- Push for resolution of issues on the agenda; do not let items remain unresolved.

- Before adjournment, summarize the results and evaluate the overall meeting effectiveness with the attendees.

- If an additional meeting is required, then set the agenda and date; solicit agreement from attendees before adjourning the current meeting.

- Within one to two days, send out the meeting minutes to the attendees, being sure to note the date and time of the next meeting within the minutes.

- The frequency of status meetings should be based upon the duration of project activities. Status review meetings should be scheduled no longer than one to two weeks after the completion of milestones, so the results can be evaluated quickly.

Every project plan should include a Communication Plan, reflecting all formal communication requirements in support of the project's stakeholders, which include the sponsors, the team, and the customers. Below is a sample of the headings for a typical communication plan:

Communication Plan				
Project name				
Project Manager Name				
Recipient	Type of Information	Frequency	Distribution Method	Report Name
[Stakeholder1]	[Description of types of information]	[daily, weekly, monthly]	[Paper, fax, email, website]	[Name of the report containing the information]
[Shareholder2]				

Project communication includes *reporting*. Reporting is a part of the communication plan and the plan should outline all reports, their objectives, their frequency, and a list of recipients.

A communication plan should also include an *escalation procedure,* which should identify who is to be contacted under identified, special circumstances or in the absence of default contacts. The escalation procedure should also include all contact information for the appropriate contacts listed in the procedure, which should include internal, direct, mobile, and pager numbers. If a contact has an administrative support resource, he or she should be listed as an alternate for that person.

Keeping everyone informed and involved within a project increases the prospect for a successful project. *Communication* is our Priority number Three for a more effective enterprise Project Management discipline.

PRIORITY FOUR -
ACCOUNTABILITY

*A*ccountability means different things to different people, but the most accepted understanding is that someone will be *answerable* to others for his or her actions. In many Project Management disciplines, there are adequate levels of documented responsibility for a project, but there is often a severe lack of *accountability* within the project. I was once told by a Project Manager that "I have never missed a due date." After sitting in on a few project status meetings, it became clear to me that the Project Manager had a pattern of changing the due dates on the tasks without being challenged. That is an example of a lack of *accountability*.

No matter what our role or responsibility, we should be held accountable for our actions. An effective Project Management discipline must include a process for handling accountability. I believe that responsibility and accountability are attached at the hip; they are a matched set of attributes found in every role within the organization and definitely within the Project Management discipline. We have heard so often that people want more responsibility but they do not want the associated accountability. Why is that? Accountability is often thought of as the negative side of having responsibility.

I believe it is inherent in an organization that responsibility carries more weight than accountability. All the positives come from successful contributions (bonuses, promotions, accolades, etc.), but the accountability for unsuccessful results is often diluted to the excuses for such undesirable results, and then everyone moves on to the next project. That next project will probably end up with the same undesirable result, as well. This dilution of accountability is usually caused by the corporation's culture more than by a lack of understanding as to how responsibility and accountability should work together.

Emphasizing responsibility and accountability is a critical factor for having an effective Project Management discipline.

Responsibility is a matter of understanding the *what, when, where, how and how much* a position is obligated to manage within the enterprise. Responsibilities are the parameters for the jurisdiction of a given position within the project; whether a Project Manager or team member, everyone has responsibilities.

Accountability means that each participant in the project knows what his or her responsibilities are and that each must answer for the actions taken while performing these responsibilities. It is the responsibility of the Program or Project Manager to ensure that every member of a project team has a clear set of responsibilities and that each one knows that each team member is being held accountable for the results within those responsibilities. To back up the Project Manager, it is the responsibility of the corporation's executive management and the program or project sponsor to ensure that the Project Manager knows his or her responsibilities and accountabilities, as well.

Accountability without repercussions is not accountability. There must be repercussions for negative actions or results. Since we are dealing with people, it is always important to keep in mind that the *objective of accountability is to reinforce the positive actions desired*, not an opportunity to demean or injure anyone. A few

examples of repercussions that can be used to reinforce accountability are as follows:

- Mentoring Approach - A one-on-one meeting to evaluate negative results and to explain and show how the
person should have acted to prevent any repetition of
the negative results. This approach is usually used for
first-timers (those showing negative tendencies for the
first time). There should be a balance between point-
ing out the negative and scrutiny of the actions while
keeping the person motivated – not only to continue his
or her duties on the current project in a positive manner, but for future projects, as well. In all approaches,
make sure to inform this person's manager if he or she
is on loan from another group or he or she works for a
subcontractor.

- Headmaster Approach - A one-on-one meeting for the
evaluation of the negative results and to review the
expected actions and results. A written Productivity
Improvement Plan for the recipient should reflect the
actions to be taken, the due dates, and desired measurable results to be accomplished. This approach is
implemented for personnel with repeated negative tendencies on projects.

- Displacement Approach - A one-on-one meeting to
review negative results and define the acceptable
expected actions and results – and to inform the person
that he is being removed from the program or project
and reassigned to other duties. This approach is implemented for a person who has either successfully completed a Productivity Improvement Plan but continues
to produce negative results or one who has failed to
complete the Productivity Improvement Plan satisfacto-
rily. The person is reassigned to other duties because

the Project Manager or operating management feels he has a skill set that can be useful to the enterprise in another capacity.

- Termination Approach - A one-on-one meeting to review the negative results and define the acceptable expected actions and results – and to inform the person that due to her inability to improve her performance after several attempts to help her make improvements, she is being terminated by the enterprise. This action is taken only if the person does not have skills that can be useful to the enterprise in another capacity.

These team mates, *Responsibility and Accountability*, are crucial to the Project Management discipline to maintain order and to provide the level of incentive for consistent, positive results that are necessary for any program or project to be completed successfully. Without the incentive of accountability to accompany responsibility, there is no emphasis on meeting deliverables as planned. If deliverables are not accomplished as planned, then the program or project will not be successful as planned. Therefore, the project becomes more costly, ends up being delivered late (if at all), and may not meet the sponsor's requirements. The important role that *Accountability* plays in the effective Project Management discipline is why it is selected as our Priority number Four.

PRIORITY FIVE – PROCESS

Process is often seen as the most critical issue in the Project Management discipline definition. This is where I disagree and why I have written this book; hopefully, that is why you are reading it. Do I think Process is important? Of course, I do. Do I think the Project Management Institute's Project Management Book of Knowledge is the Holy Grail of the Project Management discipline? Not at all! There are other sources outside the Project Management Institute organization that promote Project Management discipline methodologies and processes.

Do I think *Process* provides a structured knowledge base that is extremely helpful to an enterprise and to Project Manager's? Yes, I do! All programs or projects require a degree of structure in order to be successful and the level of structure is dependent on the type and size of the project. There is no question that the culture of the organization will have a profound effect on that organization's Project Management discipline, regardless of the type of process they have implemented. However, *because of the need for structure, Process is one of our priorities for an effective Project Management discipline.*

There are libraries full of publications defining the many Project Management processes. Our objective here is to outline the key factors that an effective Project Management discipline will contain. Each corporation will deploy the method and level of sophistication that they feel works best for the types of projects they sponsor and the capabilities of their Project Management team personnel. Our key formula for a successful project is that we maintain a *balance between the project deliverable, the project cost, and the project duration* in comparison to the project plan – while meeting the sponsor's (customer's) expectations.

It is the process that provides the structure of the project life cycle – defined as *Initiating, Planning, Executing, Monitoring/ Controlling and Closing* (Project Management Institute's Process Groups). Let's identify the key characteristics of an effective Project Management discipline process:

- *Initiating* is the beginning stage of any project and should include the definition, justification, and approval of the project.

- *Definition* - This step is comprised of a general description of the issue or condition that inspired the project, the desired deliverable or results from the project, the duration of the project, and the impacts on the enterprise once the project is complete. Depending on the size of the project and the enterprise's Project Management culture, this *definition* may be a precursor to the development of the Statement of Work – also known as the Project Scope Statement, which would be developed in the Planning stage. Otherwise, it is the Statement of Work that is used in the planning stage.

- *Justification* - Here, we have a description of the cost-benefit analysis to the enterprise for investing in this project. Included are a description of estimated benefits (material and immaterial) and costs (real and deferred), organizational and market impacts, efficiencies, and changes in business processes that are impacted by the project, just to name a few examples.

- *Approval* - Sponsorship refers to the executive and operations management that have secured the approval and financing to proceed with the project. The sponsorship should prepare a *Charter Statement*, an official document that is distributed to all project stakeholders, reflecting the sponsor's support of the project– including a brief description of the project, reference to the benefits to the enterprise, naming the Project Manager and other key positions, and the effective start and completion dates.

- *Planning* is the process whereby the project plan is defined in greater detail using the Charter Statement and the Project Definition or Statement of Work, which was completed during the initiating stage as a guideline. The project plan defines the project *stakeholders, organization structure and responsibilities, deliverables, communications plan, risk management, change management, and detailed cost-benefit analysis/control.*

  Once the project team is in place and the project plan is completed, the next step in the planning stage is to further break down the project's activities into their lowest level of components; this is called the Detail Process Flow, Work Breakdown Structure, or Task List. This Task List is then used to validate the initial cost-benefit analysis by estimating the cost and resource requirements for the project at this lower component level and to identify the critical path components that need to be acted on within the project. Let's take a brief look at the components making up the *planning* stage:

  ▫ Stakeholders - These are all the personnel who have a vested interest in the project, including executive management, operations management, Program/ Project management, project team membership, vendor/suppliers, and customers. The Project Manager should have a list reflecting each stakeholder and his or her role and requirements for the project. Stakeholder responsibilities could be project activity responsibilities or a part of the communication plan.

▫ Organization Structure and Responsibilities - Depending on the enterprise, there are several organizational structures that can be applied to a project. Larger organizations have dedicated Project Managers, project team members by operating skill sets, and separate Project Management Offices (Organizations).. Smaller organizations rely on existing operating personnel to staff the project by using some form of a matrix organization structure. Regardless of the organizational structure, the Project Manager should create a responsibility matrix which documents a list of major activities on one axis and a list of stakeholders on the other axis. Using a coding scheme, identify each stakeholder's responsibility for each intersecting activity (e.g. R=Responsible, A=Approve, C=Consult, I=Inform).

▫ Project Managers could be fully dedicated to projects, but some or all team members may be on loan from other operating organizations to the project.

▫ Deliverable - A listing of the approved deliverables or results from each activity defined in the Statement Of Work and the Work Breakdown Structure should be described and reflected in a <u>measurable</u> way. Each deliverable should be able to be tracked and must be measurable. Non-quantifiable or *soft* deliverables leave too much to interpretation and will only increase the risk of a project delay or failure later into the project. Make sure that all the stakeholders have a clear understanding of the deliverables, who is responsible for each deliverable, and approve them as defined by the project plan.

▫ Communication Plan - Since Communications was Priority number Three, I believe we have covered this topic adequately in that earlier section.

▫ Risk Management - This is the establishment of a method for identifying, assessing, and taking action on issues that pose a risk to the project. Some of the risks are known and some are unknown. The risk management process is used throughout the project from planning through to the closing. The structure for the risk management method involves a process which includes the following:

- Identify the risk

- Review and prioritize the risk based on its potential impact and probability that it may actually occur

- Create a response to the risk (ignore, postpone, or take action)

- Document risk, action taken, and communicate action taken to project team

- Continually evaluate risk throughout the project

- Establish a contingency fund to cover unforeseen expenditure

▫ Change Management - This is the development of a process for controlling change that occurs during the project. The process provides for documenting change requests from the project team, evaluating the impact of the change request, providing justification and approval/rejection of the change request, and the integration of the approved change into the overall project plan for execution.

- ▫ Financial Management - Detailed cost-benefit and financial-management controls are very important to the project process. The Project Manager may manage the expenditures in comparison to the plan (budget), or this oversight may be identified as the responsibility of an operating function, such as the accounting and finance division/department. Project Manager's should be very conscious of the financial side of the project. When risk and change issues arise, they will most certainly impact the financial side of the project, either favorably or unfavorably.

- Execution is the process of working the project plan. The Project Manager works with each of the stakeholders to ensure that the required resources (labor, equipment, systems, facilities, etc.) are available and the activities identified in the planning phase are being addressed and completed by the project team in concert with the project plan in an effective manner. The activities defined in the planning stage are now implemented for the handling of risk, communications (including reporting and meetings), and handling of change.

- Monitoring/Controlling - As one would expect, this process involves the measuring and monitoring of the overall activities being conducted in the execution stage and tracking variances to the project plan and the financial plan. The methods developed during the planning phase (communication, risk management, change management and deliverable identification) are employed to monitor and control what is being accomplished within the project.

The *variance analysis* of these monitoring processes is an ongoing activity and the mainspring for taking action to correct those issues generating the variances and thereby putting the project back on track with the project plan. In those cases where issues cannot be corrected and have an impact on the project plan, the plan is then re-fore-casted, and the new activities are added to the plan. This plan change is then documented as to the reasons for the issue, the approval of action taken, and the impact on the overall project or components affected.

Closing - Closing is an administrative process of documenting the results of the completed project, gaining acceptance (sign-offs) from all key stakeholders, and consolidating all the final documentation and reports for archiving for future reference.

The *Process* is the structure that provides the detailed plans and the direction for how to execute the project plan, and that is why it is our Priority number Five of an enterprise Project Management discipline.

ADVANCED METHODS

There are a number of new Project Management methods that have become more main stream, especially in the software and web-development industry. In case you may not have heard of them, here are a few examples: Agile, Cleanroom, DSDM, Iterative, RAD, RUP, Spiral, XP, Scrum, and V-model. Most of us are probably more familiar with the traditional *waterfall* approach, where you have a plan and a schedule for each stage and each stage must be completed before the next step can begin. However, there is strong evidence that these new methods are effective in producing a quality product or service within a shorter time frame than traditional methods.

I believe that these approaches are derivatives of the Lean movement, which revolutionized the automotive manufacturing process in Japan and has had a profound impact on all types of manufacturing throughout Japan, the USA, the EU, Australia, and to a limited degree in China. The key ideal is that there is a culture of continual improvement in every area of the enterprise and suppliers/vendors. The premise is to squeeze out every element of inefficiency, as well as non-value items and to create standard units of product or service production.

Key factors of these new methods are the breakdown of components into very small tasks or activities, meeting frequently to track results, prototyping (build versus plan), and less formality during the project process. The primary objective is to develop a product or service in the shortest period of time possible and forego the formality. Delegating of responsibility and problem resolution, using informal communications, and emphasizing a collaborative work style within the team are common attributes of these methods.

Looking at the activities conducted by the Project Manager of projects using these methods, I believe you will find that the same processes (*Initiating, Planning, Executing, Monitoring/Controlling, and Closing*) are still performed but less formally. There are greater pressures on the Project Manager of these types of projects to maintain an element of control and the ability to report project performance. Many of the organizations that are adopting these methods are more progressive in their culture, and they are more willing to take the risks associated with having less formal processes to gain the trade-off of having a product or service delivered more quickly.

CONCLUSION

Over many years, I have seen projects of all types and sizes that were managed with a variety of methods. Most of them had a reasonable level of process formality and yet the results (project success) were mixed. Not all the project failures were due to the lack of a process but more to the lack of direction, good communication, lack of accountability, and sometimes even events outside the control of the project team. Corporations have been known to cancel projects due to a change in business strategy or unforeseen events.

I continue to see evidence of a lack of understanding on the part of organizations of all sizes as to what it takes to have an effective Project Management discipline. These patterns range from Fortune 100 technology corporations to early-stage private companies. There is a movement to expand the importance of the Project Management skill set. I believe this push comes from the supply side of this new discipline (academia and associations) rather than from the demand side (corporations).

Enterprises are becoming more aware of the importance of a Project Management discipline to their *overall* performance, but they are very slow to adopt this premise. It is my opinion that corporations who demand the formal certification of Project

Managers as a requisite for employment because the supply side primarily stresses the *process* part of the Project Management discipline have learned a costly lesson. Companies now realize, as I do, that just because a Project Manager knows the Project Management discipline *process* is no guarantee that he or she can manage a project to a successful completion.

In choosing a Project Manager, the value of the right kind of leader cannot be overestimated. This is the individual who has the inherent ability and knowledge to gather together the best possible team, who will ensure that stakeholders know what is happening at all levels of the project, who sees to it that checks and balances are built in to keep the team performing to expectation, who follows a certain set of procedures to make sure the team stays on course until they reach the end goal – a satisfied sponsor or customer.

To achieve a successful project outcome, we know that we need *Leadership, Resources, Communications, Accountability and a Process*. What most enterprises do not know is that these factors are not all equal to the establishment of an *effective* Project Management discipline; they must be *prioritized*.

ABOUT THE AUTHOR

Robert Nitschke is Author of the highly regarded book *Creating A Collaborative Enterprise-Retool Your Organization To Dominate Your Markets*. He is currently founder and managing partner of CollaborationHQ LLC, an independent consulting firm providing operations management and execution support, and mentoring services to clients, nationally and internationally. His recognized for his familiar quote "Don't confuse efforts with results".

Robert's decades of relentless drive to achieve remarkable results by introducing a collaboration mindset and a focus on continuous improvement have gained him the respect of his clients, associates and peers. His extraordinary work ethic and desire to be an organizational problem solver continues to provide him with the tenacity and drive to serve where problem issues or initiatives dwell.

Robert has more than four decades of business experience, spanning a wide range of skills, experiences and industries. He has held executive and managerial positions in operations and information technology within several Fortune 500 companies and has invested over fifteen years in support of turnaround and early stage entrepreneurial ventures. Robert's results driven spirit has produced successes in telecommunication, manufacturing, ecommerce, International project finance, cruise-tour and service enterprises.

Robert is a continual learner. He is a graduate of the University of Washington, the highly recognized Tepper School of Business at Carnegie Mellon University, and holds Professional Certifications in Lean Operations and Project Management. He is proud to have served in the United States Army Security Agency and is a veteran of the Viet Nam Campaign. He is a public speaker, a blogger, teaches through teleseminars and webinars and sits on the Boards of Advisors for local companies.

To know more about Robert L. Nitschke, visit:

http://www.linkedin.com/in/rnitschke
http://www.facebook.com/CollaborationHQ
http://www.twitter.com/CollaborationHQ
hjttp://www.CollaborationHQ.com

www.ingramcontent.com/pod-product-compliance
Lightning Source LLC
Chambersburg PA
CBHW051252170526
45165CB00004B/1675